From Rejection to Love
(and other poems)

A collection of poetry with comments by the author

Judena Klebs

Introduction

This collection of poetry came out of deep canyons of my heart and mind. Some of the poetry came out of moments of tremendous despair or frustration. Much of it came out of the struggle to connect with other people. Connecting with others was very difficult for me because of the emotional damage done to me and to my ability to communicate and be understood.

Relationships are a theme you will find often in this poetry. God and His intervention in the struggling mind and emotions is another theme. My hope is that these poems will help those with emotional damage to express their needs and for counselors and friends to understand those needs.

After each poem, I comment, line by line, about the poem that was just printed. This is for clarification of some of the meaning, especially symbolism which many may not understand. I hope this book will be a textbook of learning in order to bridge the gap between those who are wounded and those who long to help them.

Judena Klebs

FROM REJECTION TO LOVE

There is a road many miles long
To travel upon it, one must be strong
To endure the threats along the way
And be careful upon the path to stay
So the wild beasts don't destroy you there
Or you never arrive because of fear
It winds around many a rocky place
And the wind blows hard upon your face
Your feet may stumble, your knees grow weak
And the chances for reaching your goal seem bleak
But travel you must, though the night closes in
Though your vision becomes foggy and your hopes grow thin
You'll be given just enough light from above
If you're willing to travel from rejection to love

FROM REJECTION TO LOVE (author's comments)

There is a road many miles long

(The road is long because the more damage which has been done to a person, the more ground has to be covered, erasing the influence of rejection in his or her life and preparing that person to accept love.)

To travel upon it, one must be strong

(The road is not easy. Those who travel it must be strong and determined inwardly in order to overcome the difficulties. They must have power and energy to be persistent.)

To endure the threats along the way

(There are spiritual, emotional, mental, and even physical obstacles which threaten to be a stumbling block if any of the steps toward wellness do not prepare for enemies to one's mental health. Realistically, expect opposition to be there.)

And be careful upon the path to stay

(One cannot be detoured from the path because the elements needed toward health may not be found in denial.)

So the wild beasts don't destroy you there

(The "wild beasts" are emotions which become out of control because of the thoughts which the person has been brainwashed to believe about themself and the world. They destroy hope and self-esteem, threatening to conquer a person's mind.)

Or you never arrive because of fear

(Fear can be such an overwhelming and crippling emotion. It stops us in our path and possibly causes us to run in the wrong direction, never arriving at the help we seek.)

It winds around many a rocky place

(There are real dangers as one tries to move forward toward the ability to receive love. So much of the world rejects us and discourages us from believing that there is anything better. So we give up hope.)

And the wind blows hard upon your face

(There are many forms of resistance in a hostile world. We struggle to go forward. Hopelessness or self-pity may stop us from progressing.)

Your feet may stumble, your knees grow weak

(Although we may be determined to travel, if we are not firmly grounded in a new reality, our feet will stumble. Our foundation could cave in. Our knees are what give us balance. We totter. We cannot keep ourselves going in the right direction if the joints of knowledge about ourselves cannot produce determination and strength.)

And the chances for reaching your goal seem bleak

(At any point along the way, hopelessness or a lack of enlightenment concerning our goal can make the journey seem impossible.)

But travel you must, though the night closes in

(There is no other option if one is to survive than to get from the rejection mode to the love mode. If one does not persist while able, time will bring darkness upon the path and make it harder to see truth and reach the goal.)

Though your vision becomes foggy and your hopes grow thin

(The less we see the path clearly, the less hope will be available for us to continue.)

You'll be given just enough light from above

(The light comes only step-by-step for that person who is only familiar with rejection.)

If you're willing to travel from rejection to love

(Only true willingness will lead you forward. You will arrive at the opposite of rejection, which is love.)

TOO MUCH LOVE

Too much love you gave to me
More love than I thought could ever be
I looked but did not understand
What I was holding in my hand
I turned it 'round and 'round to see
But only love stared back at me
I tried to tear that love apart
To peer inside and find its heart
But to its heart I found no key
For it was pure reality
I turned away and quickened my stride
I desperately searched for a place to hide
For fear love should take its hold on me
For fear love should come and set me free
I found no refuge from its heat
The blisters burned my running feet
I crouched behind hate's iron door
And screamed at love "No more! No more!

Please send your face away from me
For I am afraid of the love I see!"
But love ignored my troubled cry
For love was love and it had to try
At last it took me in its arms
And my soul was arrested by its charms
I felt a strange new warmth within
And the walls of fear were wearing thin
There were a few more efforts to squirm away
Then the fire blazed to the light of day
I slowly opened my dazzled eyes
And, one by one, dropped each disguise
Love took my hand and helped me through
And then it led me back to you
Now, too much love for you I share
More love than my heart can ever bear
So, don't be surprised at my frequent plea
"Here, take some of this love from me!"

TOO MUCH LOVE (author's comments)

Too much love you gave to me

(This love that you seem to be offering to me is overwhelming because I am not used to it. Even though I always wished to be loved, I never learned how to accept it, so it frightens me. Surely, this love is more than a person like me could tolerate. It is foreign to life as I know it.)

More love than I thought could ever be

(I wasn't expecting love to be so great, therefore, once again, I am not used to it. Love like this could never be meant for someone like me who feels so bad about herself.)

I looked but did not understand

(You gave the love to me but I did not recognize it for what it was.)

What I was holding in my hand

(In a sense, I had accepted it because symbolically, I held it.)

I turned it 'round and 'round to see

(I tried to investigate what I had, hoping that with my limited emotional eyesight, I could identify its nature.)

But only love stared back at me

(No matter how I had tried to imagine what this object was, to the point of suspicion, its real nature continued to look me in the eye.)

I tried to tear that love apart

(Since observation had not explained anything new to me, I began to try taking this gift apart. This I could do by acting unlovable to see if the love would disintegrate. I could also find various other ways to reject the love and see whether it would last or not.)

To peer inside and find its heart

(Now curiosity about this strange object has me trying to open it up and guess what the motive is behind it.)

But to its heart I found no key

(There was no explanation for love being what it was and no ulterior motive that I could uncover.)

For it was pure reality

(The love was sincere. I could find nothing behind it.)

I turned away and quickened my stride

(If I couldn't guess away the nature of the love, I would begin to run from it. Its reality is frightening to one inexperienced by it.)

I desperately searched for a place to hide

(Hiding from love also comes from a lack of understanding of its nature. Everything else in life has hurt me so far. Love must be something else to hurt me, something I should greatly fear.)

For fear love should take its hold on me

(At this point, I am afraid of the harm that might come to me if love gets the upper hand.)

For fear love should come and set me free

(I also fear that by freeing me, love will toss me into the unknown. Would I be free of my familiar pain which has become a "security blanket"? What exactly is freedom for me?)

I found no refuge from its heat

(Love has a warmth to it that is frightening for one who has been "burned" by other types of "heat", such as emotional pain and injury.)

The blisters burned my running feet

(There is pain in running from love as well as in accepting it because the desire to be loved is strong, at least as strong as the fear of it.)

I crouched behind hate's iron door

(At this point, the fear becomes disguised as hatred. I need something strong to protect me from this strange experience. I begin to push others away with my false hatred.)

And screamed at love "No more! No more!

(Now the fear becomes more intense. I am not able to hide the fear any longer.)

Please send your face away from me

(Love has a face. It is shown through the eyes and mouth, as well as the expression, itself, on one's face. I am confronted with love directly when I see it on a face.)

For I am afraid of the love I see!"

(It is the love I see on the face of the one who loves me that frightens me. For when I see it, I must respond to it in some way.)

But love ignored my troubled cry

(Love knows better than to pay attention to cries of fear. It continues on and recognizes the true cry for help behind the fear.)

For love was love and it had to try

(The nature of love is that it persists and never gives up on the loved one.)

At last it took me in its arms

(The persistence of love progresses from the face to the arms. The arms are for comfort and protection. The caring aspect of love finally envelops me.)

And my soul was arrested by its charms

(No longer can my soul run in fear from love because love's benefits are grabbing my attention, forcing me to face my need for love and revealing my value to me.)

I felt a strange new warmth within

(Now the love is penetrating into my inner self and the heat I was originally afraid of is a comforting and healing type of warmth.)

And the walls of fear were wearing thin

(The fear is still there but the healing balm of love is wearing away the walls I had erected to protect myself from this foreign object.)

There were a few more efforts to squirm away

(The battle with fear of love is slowly dying. Only a little struggle still remains.)

Then the fire blazed to the light of day

(Eventually, love presents itself in full illumination.)

I slowly opened my dazzled eyes

(As strange and new as this experience is, eventually the inner eyes adjust to seeing its fullness for the first time.)

And, one by one, dropped each disguise

(No longer can I fool myself or others that I don't want or need their love.)

Love took my hand and helped me through

(Love, itself, guides a person in how to accept it, no matter how long that process may take.)

And then it led me back to you

(Love, eventually, longs to reciprocate to the person who gave the love to begin with.)

Now, too much love for you I share

(It is just as overwhelming now to be on the giving side of love.)

More love than my heart can ever bear

(The love cannot be contained. It must be given out.)

So, don't be surprised at my frequent plea

(The giving of love overflows so that its expression comes repeatedly.)

"Here, take some of this love from me!"

(The giving of love becomes an urgent need.)

AN OPEN BOOK

My life is now an open book
Where one like you can take a look
The cover, once sealed tight, has been
Pried open by trust so hard to win
The pages are torn, the edges marred,
The print somewhat blurred and the binding scarred
A story sad is held inside
Hidden from those with scorn or pride
Who might rip the pages even more
But, for you, I open up the door
Not many are allowed to take a look
Inside this life, inside this book
But trust unclasped it like a key
So eyes of love could look and see
So eyes of love could read and know
How to finish the book and help me grow
Be a part of the story, be a part of me
Write new words of love for me to see
You're invited inside to write new themes,
To start a new chapter, help me find new dreams
The story is now about you, too
With a different touch, a different view
To give it an eternally different end
Than if you had never become my friend
So read and write and let me be
An open book eternally

AN OPEN BOOK (author's comments)

My life is now an open book

(To be transparent and reveal things about one's self and life does not come immediately. But I have arrived at that point and am announcing it to those I trust.)

Where one like you can take a look

(I select one or more persons to be able to see what has been hidden for so long.)

The cover, once sealed tight, has been

(Once the cover was so tightly closed that no one could see the hurts and scars of the past.)

Pried open by trust so hard to win

(Trust is a difficult thing to give to others when one has been hurt repeatedly. Amazingly, it has been won by the faithful love of another.)

The pages are torn, the edges marred,

(Life has torn and marred what could have been contained in this book. My story would not have had to be so sad if not damaged by others who have had access to my soul and all that has been told about it in this book.)

The print somewhat blurred and the binding scarred

(It is hard to read some parts of this book because its expression has been hindered by the rejection contained in it. The binding which holds my story together has been scarred through trauma.)

A story sad is held inside

(Heartbreak, depression, despair, and emotional pain are all held inside the book and are part of its story.)

Hidden from those with scorn or pride

(The story has been hidden from those who would scorn or make fun of my pain and from those who think they are better than me because they have not suffered in the same ways.)

Who might rip the pages even more

(The scornful or prideful are likely to have damaged me further.)

But, for you, I open up the door

(You have earned a special place in my heart that I would dare to trust you.)

Not many are allowed to take a look

(Only very few are given permission to see what is inside.)

Inside this life, inside this book

(This book of my life contains my story which is my soul.)

But trust unclasped it like a key

(Only trust could open this mysterious book.)

So eyes of love could look and see

(Only the spiritual eyes of those who love me could find true meaning in my story.)

So eyes of love could read and know

(Only those loving, spiritual eyes would learn to understand the true content and nature of my life.)

How to finish the book and help me grow

(Now the purpose of exposing my story to the ones I trust is revealed. Those people will be a part of the ending to my story and helpful in guiding me to use my experiences to mature more fully.)

Be a part of the story, be a part of me

(Begin to interact with my life to make a difference in my story and to change my condition as you relate to my life.)

Write new words of love for me to see

(Your love adds quality to my life's story. The love will be revealed to me as you add your own personality and "flavor" to my life.)

You're invited inside to write new themes,

(The extended meaning in my life is now up to you as you add your own creative ideas to my life.)

To start a new chapter, help me find new dreams

(New life will come into my story as you add inspiration and ideas for new goals.)

The story is now about you, too

(You are in my life and I am in yours as we interact. It tells a lot about you as well as me.)

With a different touch, a different view

(You add your unique mind and personality to my story. What you believe helps make the difference for me.)

To give it an eternally different end

(You help to write the ending and outcome of my story.)

Than if you had never become my friend

(The ending would be far different without your friendship.)

So read and write and let me be

(Participate in my story with me.)

An open book eternally

(Help me to keep the book open forever and don't give me reason to close my life to you.)

MY JOURNEY TO YOU

Once I could not see
That you needed me
We both longed for the day
When I would be free
As time passed by
We both wondered why
I never seemed to care
While deep inside
My spirit cried
To reach out and to share
I tried to see where I had been wrong
Why my life had been singing such an empty song
My world had been closing in on me
And I searched to find reality
As soon as I dared to step closer to you
I saw you were needing my friendship, too
This made things even harder to bear
I tried to let you see my tear

That would show you the love that I couldn't give
Until I could find the way to live
But it didn't help, it didn't relieve
For love was still there that we couldn't receive
As I learned the things that I needed to know
My progress came but so very slow
I didn't think you would wait for me
But you not only waited, you gave me the key
As I opened the door, my heart gave way
For there was yet another price to pay
But when I was spent and that price had been paid
I knew that a worthy investment was made
So now as I enter, I have much to say
I have so much to give and so much to relay
I want you to know what you now mean to me
I want you to see that at last I am free

MY JOURNEY TO YOU (author's comments)

Once I could not see
That you needed me

(When one's self-esteem is very low, they are unable to imagine that others could need them in any way. They may not even realize that they have the power to hurt others just as they have been hurt or to influence them in a good way. How can you have power to affect others for good or ill if you have no value as a person?)

We both longed for the day
When I would be free

(The need for one another is mutual, creating the longing to be free to relate to one another. Each person must be liberated from what causes them to isolate from the other. This could be a hindrance from either end or from both ends. The poem expresses the realization that one's own personal inhibition has caused a gap.)

As time passed by
We both wondered why
I never seemed to care

(It appears that I am rejecting another and they may interpret my behavior that way. But I, also, do not understand my own behavior. I did care but did not understand why I could not show it.)

While deep inside
My spirit cried
To reach out and to share

(There is frustration in the inner being because the love within me longs to reach out to the other.)

I tried to see where I had been wrong

(Could this barrier be my fault? Is there anything I could be doing differently?)

Why my life had been singing such an empty song

(The vacuum in my soul created by the absence of true friends causes whatever expression of my life to be empty.)

My world had been closing in on me

(How could I relate to other people when my own world of hurt was so overwhelming that it was suffocating me?)

And I searched to find reality

(I was so lost in my own search that I could not read your concern for me.)

As soon as I dared to step closer to you

(Though afraid, I began to draw closer)

I saw you were needing my friendship, too

(It is hard to imagine that you needed me since my self-esteem was so low that I thought I had nothing to offer. But when I drew nearer, I saw the need in your eyes.)

This made things even harder to bear

(Knowing that you've been needing me the whole time and that I had let you down made the anguish of being separated from you more severe.)

I tried to let you see my tear

(My pain was barely visible from the outside of me because I was "clammed up", trying to protect myself. Perhaps, if you see even one tear, you will understand that I care.)

That would show you the love that I couldn't give

(Behind that tear, there is love that I could not show. Just a little sign of love through my pain may relieve your feelings that I have no interest in you and your needs.)

Until I could find the way to live

(Until my own needs could be met and a path for my own life be opened up, I could not begin to adequately meet your need for mutual companionship.)

But it didn't help, it didn't relieve

(Such an effort to express my love was too inadequate.)

For love was still there that we couldn't receive

(Not only could I not give the love to you that my heart contained, but I could not open up to your love either.)

As I learned the things that I needed to know

(Gradually, new light concerning the truths about both of us began to shine on the path I followed toward you.)

My progress came, but so very slow

(As I journeyed toward you, I felt impatient because I did not want you to give up on me. And I was also frustrated with myself.)

I didn't think you would wait for me

(If you were to become impatient, like so many others, it would devastate me.)

But you not only waited, you gave me the key

(It not only requires your patience but the way in which you reach out to me so that I can grab a hold on a tangible way to trust you. It takes some initiative on your part to reach out to me in such a way that I can see the evidence of your love.)

As I opened the door, my heart gave way

(Thinking I had found my help in your love by opening the door to receive it, I found that relationships are complicated and this frightened me.)

For there was yet another price to pay

(Now I saw that not only must I receive that love, but learn how to give love back in return.)

But when I was spent and that price had been paid

(I found out that to give love, I must give my very self away.)

I knew that a worthy investment was made

(Love, by its very nature, values the loved one absolutely.)

So now as I enter, I have much to say

(This is where true communication begins. Once the self is spent for the other in commitment of some sort, the expression of love comes about. This may be said in words but always will be said in actions as well.)

I have so much to give and so much to relay

(The self flows with the expression of love.)

I want you to know what you now mean to me

(The one who loves wants the loved one to know their worth to them.)

I want you to see that at last I am free

(My openness to you is now apparent and the relationship takes on a healthy balance. As you see my freedom to receive love, you can enjoy my ability to love you as well.)

JUST "WHAT I AM"

Just "what I am" I offer to you
I have nothing more and nothing less will do
I cannot give what I do not own
Yet there is no end to the love I would loan
If I only could show what my heart would say,
If, for all the love I know, I could find a way
To give it to you
That's just what I'd do
But I have only "me" to set before you and say,
"Take this. It's yours. Let me give it away."
Take whatever there may be inside of me
Take whatever has been planted as it grows to a tree
While eternity passes, it will grow there for you
You will watch it forever. It will always be new
This is all I can promise, my only guarantee
"You will never be sorry that you held on for me."
But I have nothing more and nothing less will do
So just "what I am" I offer to you

JUST "WHAT I AM" (author's comments)

Just "what I am" I offer to you

(I give my self to you.)

I have nothing more and nothing less will do

(One cannot give more than their very self. Anything more is not really the true self. Anything less is not true commitment.)

I cannot give what I do not own

(It would be hypocritical to offer qualities that I have not truly made a part of my self.)

Yet there is no end to the love I would loan

(I hold nothing back, however, of the love available for me to give.)

If I only could show what my heart would say,

(Even though my willingness to love is endless, the expression part of it holds me back.)

If, for all the love I know, I could find a way

(Out of any of my own understanding of love, I wish I could find a way to give that love to you.)

To give it to you

(I want to invest my love in you)

That's just what I'd do

(My will is completely involved in being able to express love.)

But I have only "me" to set before you and say,

(Everything "boils down" to the simple giving of my self.)

"Take this. It's yours. Let me give it away."

(Through my commitment to love you, my self now belongs to you.)

Take whatever there may be inside of me

(Every good quality I have is ready to be received by you.)

Take whatever has been planted as it grows to a tree

(Everything good in me has been planted by God. It will continue to grow larger.)

While eternity passes, it will grow there for you

(The good within me will continue to grow forever and will belong to everyone in any type of relationship with me.)

You will watch it forever. It will always be new

(As my inner self develops, it will be available to observe eternally and yet it will always be refreshingly new because of the continuous change that God produces in me.)

This is all I can promise, my only guarantee

(There is only one promise I can make concerning this giving away of my self.)

"You will never be sorry that you held on for me."

(Your devotion to me will always reward you as long as you enjoy who I am.)

But I have nothing more and nothing less will do

(Once again, I realize that the only thing I can truly give another is what I have. And yet, I need to make sure that I give it completely.)

So just "what I am" I offer to you

(I give myself to you.)

THE ONE WHO BELIEVED IN ME

Because someone believed in me
I found that I, too, could be free
And in the blindness of past years
With all its emptiness and tears
Hope found its way through all my fears
Because someone believed in me

Because someone believed in me
I chose the right a little more
Though I did not know what I was standing for
I stood before the open door
Of love from the one who believed in me

Because someone showed he really cared
I persevered when I would have despaired
I fought my way through starless nights
For I could see the unfading lights
In the eyes of the one who believed in me

Because he said I would be great
He changed the outcome of my fate
I was given my future's golden key
From the hand of the one who believed in me

THE ONE WHO BELIEVED IN ME (author's comments)

Because someone believed in me

(I needed someone to have faith and confidence in my value and ability.)

I found that I, too, could be free

(The person who believed in me had to believe first in themselves to see the value in others. And now, their faith in me frees me to love myself and others.)

And in the blindness of past years

(In the past, I saw no value in myself. I was blind to my own good qualities.)

With all its emptiness and tears

(Without faith in myself, my world was empty. Not only that, but grieving and pain controlled me.)

Hope found its way through all my fears

(The other person's faith in me brought me hope which penetrated through the tremendous fear that controlled my life.)

Because someone believed in me

(I recognized that I was incapable of believing in myself at that point in my life. The person on the outside of me, taking the time to believe in me, gets credit for starting the process.)

Because someone believed in me

(Once again, I referred to the cause of my deliverance from low self-esteem.)

I chose the right a little more

(The person's faith in me influenced me to make the right choices.)

Though I did not know what I was standing for

(I was confused about the meaning of life and what I needed to do concerning my own life.)

I stood before the open door

(Even though I didn't really know what to believe in, through the other person's faith, I found myself standing in front of an amazing opportunity.)

Of love from the one who believed in me

(The other person's faith came out of their love for me. That is what opened the door for me to move on.)

Because someone showed he really cared

(The person who believed in me had to show his caring, in some way letting the love get through to me.)

I persevered when I would have despaired

(Grabbing a hold on that person's faith kept me trying to find the answers for my healing instead of giving up.)

I fought my way through starless nights

(In the world I found myself in, there was no natural light to lead me from the darkness. I could not fight my way through this darkness of my mind and emotions without some light from outside myself.)

For I could see the unfading lights

(There was a strange light to guide me that continued to shine brightly in my darkness, giving me energy and hope to fight toward it.)

In the eyes of the one who believed in me

(That light came from the spiritual eyes of someone who could see my value.)

Because he said I would be great

(This person spoke words of encouragement based on his belief in my potential for greatness.)

He changed the outcome of my fate

(The direction in which my life was heading was turned around so that my circumstances changed.)

I was given my future's golden key

(There was a key to a new future that I was able to receive.)

From the hand of the one who believed in me

(That key came from the person's active faith in my life as he handed a new future to me.)

HEALING A BROKEN HEART

When God heals a broken heart
He knows exactly where to start
Because He knows what it will take
For He sees each place the heart can break
He also knows just who to find
That He can trust to be kind
And to wipe the tears away
By gentle words that they can say

When God heals a wounded soul
He has a plan in His control
A design to win that life
Which has been broken by hurt and strife
He understands and feels the pain
When hurt has come again and again
It takes many types of glue
To fix the heart before He's through
It takes compassion, it takes prayer
It takes hearts who really care
It takes wisdom from above
Reassurance and love

When God heals a broken heart
He chooses friends who won't depart
He chooses someone just like you
Who can love the way you do
He takes the time to mend each part
When God heals a broken heart

HEALING A BROKEN HEART (author's comments)

When God heals a broken heart

(Ultimately, it is God who heals the broken heart. He is the Master Surgeon, giving orders to those He wants to work through. He works through people, but those people must obey His orders.)

He knows exactly where to start

(The broken heart is a complicated thing. Only God knows what steps to take and the order necessary to complete the job successfully.)

Because He knows what it will take

(God, in His wisdom, sees all that is needed to do the job.)

For He sees each place the heart can break

(A person's spirit and personality can be damaged along with their mind and emotions. There are many places inside a human that are injured and may need to be healed. God alone sees each part and extent of the damage.)

He also knows just who to find

(God matches people together who need each other to help produce healing.)

That He can trust to be kind

(God looks for those who are compassionate and caring. These are the only ones he can trust to do the job.)

And to wipe the tears away

(God trusts those who can bring comfort to the hurting.)

By gentle words that they can say

(Careful, sensitive words produce healing.)

When God heals a wounded soul

(The very being of a person can carry deep wounds. God looks for the opportunity to restore such a person.)

He has a plan in His control

(God has a purpose and His own way of working to fulfill His promise to heal.)

A design to win that life

(His purpose is to lead the person into His love and help.)

Which has been broken by hurt and strife

(Painful discord within relationships causes so many of the deep wounds.)

He understands and feels the pain

(God knows exactly what we are going through when we are injured.)

When hurt has come again and again

(Repeated hurt deepens the wounds more and more. Much healing is required.)

It takes many types of glue

(There are more than one or two elements involved in healing deep wounds.)

To fix the heart before He's through

(As with physical wounds, there are various medicines, each with their own purpose to serve in cleaning out the wound and healing it properly.)

It takes compassion, it takes prayer

(A true love and concern for those hurting is necessary as well as intercession for them before God.)

It takes hearts who really care

(The concern must be genuine and from the heart.)

It takes wisdom from above

(We cannot heal the heart on our own. God's wisdom and intelligence is where it all starts.)

Reassurance and love

(Insecure, wounded people need to be given a lot of reassurance along with continued love.)

When God heals a broken heart

(God continues to heal by adding even more elements to the process.)

He chooses friends who won't depart

(How many can God trust to continue to be faithful and to fulfill the role that He has given them as a healing balm for the one who is hurting?)

He chooses someone just like you

(Are you personally available to fill this role?)

Who can love the way you do

(Each of us has a unique capacity to show love in a special way.)

He takes the time to mend each part

(Patience to see each part of the wound mended is a quality of God but also one He lends to others.)

When God heals a broken heart

(Once again, the reminder is given that God is the one who heals.)

BENEATH THE GROUND

There is a well of pain
So dark and deep
Beneath the ground
Where willows weep
Filled up with tears
And too far down to see
In the depths
Of the inner parts of me

All alone in there
Are pools of despair
And of grief that cannot reach my face
By the hint of a sigh
Or by a tear that sneaks by
You might sense the slightest trace
Of the pain that's too far down to see
In the depths
Of the inner parts of me

Send down a bucket
Into the well
Bring something to the surface
Allow me to tell
Some of the things I've been afraid to say
Before vines cover the ground
And you can't find a way
To where I am hidden
Too far down to see
In the depths
Of the inner parts of me

BENEATH THE GROUND (author's comments)

There is a well of pain
So dark and deep

(The pain I feel is more obscure and deep than people realize.)

Beneath the ground
Where willows weep

(It is beneath the surface of my life. Even nature feels my pain.)

Filled up with tears
And too far down to see

(The tears are mostly hiding beneath the surface. Most people will miss observing them.)

In the depths
Of the inner parts of me

(These are in the hidden inner parts or personalities of my being.)

All alone in there
Are pools of despair

(There is no one to comfort me that far down away from friends who understand. More than one depth of hopelessness is present. There are various issues that lead to that despair in each part.)

And of grief that cannot reach my face
By the hint of a sigh
Or by a tear that sneaks by

(The sorrowful cries of my soul are so deep that the expression of that sorrow and loss does not show to others. You might notice small signs that something is wrong. You may see a tear or other sign of grief. Otherwise my pain may not show itself fully.)

You might sense the slightest trace
Of the pain that's too far down to see
In the depths

Of the inner parts of me

(Looking closely, you may see something representing my pain if you are sensitive enough. You could not even guess how much pain those simple signs that you see truly represent. It is too deep.)

Send down a bucket
Into the well

(I need help expressing myself by your love and openness reaching out to me. This requires humility on your part to reach down into depths that expose you, also, to the pain I hold.)

Bring something to the surface
Allow me to tell

(I need you to help me bring out of this well of pain some expression of my secret memories to relieve some of the pain and the frustration of keeping it all inside. Talking about my problems and horrible memories is a big key to my healing. Keeping them secret only makes their effect on me worse.)

Some of the things I've been afraid to say

(There is a dread of bringing these memories up for fear that it will be like experiencing them again or being judged for them.)

Before vines cover the ground
And you can't find a way

(Eventually, I will close up permanently if no expression is given to me to relieve my pain. Once I am covered completely, there will be no way to reach me.)

To where I am hidden
Too far down to see
In the depths
Of the inner parts of me

(I am hidden down there in my pain. You will not even be able to see me and understand all I represent if you wait too long.)

SUICIDE

There's a dark world where I can hide
A place that is called "Suicide"
Where no one can touch me or rip my heart
A place to which I long to depart
It seems so safe compared to life
To turn to pills, razor blade, or knife
Even physical pain brings a certain release
From deeper pain and brings me peace
Cut off from friends who seem like foes
Hidden away in the dark where no one knows
The secrets I am afraid to tell
Where no one can get to know me well
Because they might not really love me
If they look in the dark and can somehow see
My past and all it has done to my soul
Suicide is my last control
To choose to live means to open my life
That is worse than pain of death or knife
The risks I take are more painful for me
Than bleeding or dying could ever be

And yet I hear a voice, a call
Wooing me gently away from it all
Saying, "Give us a chance to somehow care
Come out of the dark and the dangers there."
But if I'm afraid to take your hand
Please, try somehow to understand
That it's safer here in my dark domain
Where I've found my own way to cope with pain
And forgive me for not responding to your call
When I'm able to hear your voice at all
Alone in this dark world I have made
Trying to comfort myself in its silent shade
Yet don't stop calling me out. Please, reach your hand to me
There may be a chance that I'll take it, you see
And come out of this world and come out of the night
To grasp on to some hope and continue my fight
A chance that your love will get through some way
And bring me back into the light of day
And I'll have less need to run and hide
To the world that is called "Suicide"

SUICIDE (author's comments)

There's a dark world where I can hide
A place that is called "Suicide"
Where no one can touch me or rip my heart
A place to which I long to depart

(The behavior which most people refer to as "suicide" appears to me in my emotional suffering as a place of refuge, a place to hide from those who have continued to inflict suffering and painful rejection upon me. I long to find that way of escape.)

It seems so safe compared to life
To turn to pills, razor blade, or knife
Even physical pain brings a certain release
From deeper pain and brings me peace

(The world of life has come only to mean pain and rejection. The reality that appears to be opposite of this seems to be a friend. The means to harm myself physically, such as pills, razor blade, or knife actually seem to speak safety rather than harm to me while I escape the terrible experience of life. Physical pain even brings a distraction which relieves me temporarily from the experience of emotional pain.)

Cut off from friends who seem like foes

(Whether these friends in reality truly care for me, my perspective is that everyone is an enemy which cannot be trusted.)

Hidden away in the dark where no one knows
The secrets I am afraid to tell

(To reveal anything about the past or who I am now would threaten to take away that world in which I hide. What would people do to my memories? Make them worse?)

Where no one can get to know me well
Because they might not really love me

(Others would get to know me and find out how unlovable I am.)

If they look in the dark and can somehow see
My past and all it has done to my soul

(If they could see the damage done to me, they might believe I am beyond repair and communicate that hopelessness to me. If I believe that hopelessness, it would be suicide for my soul rather than my body.)

Suicide is my last control

(I am at the point where nothing in life seems to be within my control. Making the choice to end my life is the last desperate effort to have control over my destiny for one last fleeting moment.)

To choose to live means to open my life
That is worse than pain of death or knife
The risks I take are more painful for me
Than bleeding or dying could ever be

(Opening up to the threat of someone hurting me again would be so painful that I can't imagine why harming myself physically is the problem. In reality, I cannot really solve my emotional pain permanently through self-harm. Yet my thinking is irrational due to the overwhelming pain that has been building within me for so long.)

And yet I hear a voice, a call
Wooing me gently away from it all
Saying, "Give us a chance to somehow care
Come out of the dark and the dangers there."

(There are people on the outside of my experience calling me to reconsider the path of suicide I have chosen. I begin to listen to what they are saying and question myself.)

But if I'm afraid to take your hand
Please, try somehow to understand
That it's safer here in my dark domain
Where I've found my own way to cope with pain

(Trust is a very difficult thing for me. That is why I built walls of protection against people in the first place.)

And forgive me for not responding to your call
When I'm able to hear your voice at all

(I hear my true friends part of the time when I am not consumed with pain that keeps me irrational.)

Alone in this dark world I have made
Trying to comfort myself in its silent shade

(This world is a counterfeit "safe place". Yet it only leads me toward death rather than a good life.)

Yet don't stop calling me out. Please, reach your hand to me
There may be a chance that I'll take it, you see

(In my desperation, I truly want to be rescued and given hope for a better way.)

And come out of this world, and come out of the night
To grasp on to some hope and continue my fight

(If hope is brought to me, I may have the strength to fight for my emotional health again.)

A chance that your love will get through some way
And bring me back into the light of day

(I really want the love you may be offering to me if I can discover that it is real. It is the only way I can hope to move out of my darkness into a better world.)

And I'll have less need to run and hide
To the world that is called "Suicide"

(You can help prevent me from the urge to end my life as your love draws me out of the habit of escaping into that dark world.)

SEA OF MEMORIES

Like a raging, troubled sea
Memories come flooding over me
I am sinking. Don't let me drown!
I struggle up, sorrow pushes me down
I need the love I long to find
I reach out for it and then go blind
It slips away and I think I'll die
While waves of faces go floating by
Were any of them reaching out to me?
If they were, I could not see
Or understand the words they say
They speak a language that holds no sway
Of comprehension for my heart
The pain is great. I'm torn apart
Like a boat upon the wave
Lower your ladder to my grave
Rescue me from memory's grip
Take me aboard upon your ship
Give me assurance of your love and care
Until the waters calm of my despair
Let the tempest stop its rage, its turning
While I grasp the help for which I'm yearning
And bring me to a place upon the shore
Where memories torment my mind no more

SEA OF MEMORIES (author's comments)

Like a raging, troubled sea
Memories come flooding over me

(My memories are full of angry and fearful emotions. They overwhelm me.)

I am sinking. Don't let me drown!

(The urgency to be rescued from my frightening and painful memories leads almost to a panic.)

I struggle up, sorrow pushes me down

(No matter how hard I struggle to overcome these memories, the sadness I feel keeps me so heavy, it is like someone pushing me beneath the water of despair.)

I need the love I long to find

(Love would help to boost me back up to the surface. I not only long for it, I need it to survive.)

I reach out for it and then, go blind

(Even though I reach for love, the water of memories splashes up to blind me.)

It slips away and I think I'll die

(As the love slips out of my grasp, I expect death as a result.)

While waves of faces go floating by

(The people in my life go by me in flashes.)

Were any of them reaching out to me?

(I look for a sign of love in those faces.)

If they were, I could not see

(I cannot perceive love.)

Or understand the words they say
(The words of love mean nothing to me as long as I am drowning in memories.)

They speak a language that holds no sway

(I cannot be influenced by their words for I don't understand the meaning of love.)

Of comprehension for my heart

(I can't receive any love.)

The pain is great. I'm torn apart

(The memories are painful. They tear me because there is nothing to hold me together as long as I cannot receive friendship or love to relieve me of some of the pain.)

Like a boat upon the wave
Lower your ladder to my grave

(My only hope is for someone to come along who can provide a refuge from my memories. It takes the initiative of someone stable to reach out and help the victim of traumatic memories. They must be able to reach down into that situation, understanding the feelings of the desperate person who believes they are drowning in all their pain.)

Rescue me from memory's grip

(One must understand that these memories have a strong hold on the person who is influenced by them. The person is held prisoner to what they believe about life and about themselves because of these memories.)

Take me aboard upon your ship

(Take me from my life's view and bring me to a place of stability and safety from harmful memories.)

Give me assurance of your love and care

(Love is always an essential part of helping. The one being helped cannot become stable without it.)

Until the waters calm of my despair

(The turmoil I experience will settle down and hope begins to rise.)

Let the tempest stop its rage, its turning

(As the waters, full of memories, calm around me, I am more at peace.)

While I grasp the help for which I'm yearning

(Then I can reach out and receive your help.)

And bring me to a place upon the shore

(Now I am ready for more stability.)

Where memories torment my mind no more

(At last the memories have no hold on me. I am arriving to a secure haven with your rescuing completed.)

MANY PEOPLE

There are many people
Inside of me
Struggling and crying
And yearning to be free
All desperately searching
To find their way
All longing to see
A better day
They all carry pain
They all hold grief
Only by splitting
Can they find relief
Yet relief does not last
So they divide again
While each new part
Explodes with pain
These people overwhelm me
As they crowd into my soul
No one seems to understand
That they want to be whole

But they each must be healed
And work hand in hand
Building new dreams
Out of mountains of sand
The people who have struggled
To keep my mind alive
Have divided in my soul
To help me survive
They deserve honor
Not ridicule or shame
For they hold an identity
With or without a name
So help them heal
And comfort each one
Until they all shine together
Like rays of the sun

Introduction to "MANY PEOPLE"

There is a diagnosis called Dissociative Identity Disorder (D.I.D.), formerly known as Multiple Personality Disorder (M.P.D). It is often misunderstood to be the result of demons or confused with other diagnoses.

Much of the breaking into different parts (often called personalities) is due to trauma, especially in young childhood. Because the traumatic experiences are so great, in order to keep the mind sane, many times various parts of the mind manifest themselves separately. They are designated by the mind to carry certain memories and cope with them in their own way. Various other parts of the person may manifest themselves as helpers or they may be self-destructive in some way, sabotaging the work of healing and integration.

This poem expresses my experience with the struggle that goes on in the process of healing these various parts.

MANY PEOPLE (author's comments)

There are many people
Inside of me

(My experience from young childhood was to respond to the abuse I suffered by dividing into various parts of my self. This was in order to cope with physical and emotional pain. I eventually suffered confusion as a result, not knowing who the real "me" was.)

Struggling and crying
And yearning to be free

(The various parts struggle to be healed of the memories they contain.)

All desperately searching
To find their way

(Each one is trying to figure out who they are, what role they play, and how to discover what direction they need to take to be whole with the other parts.)

All longing to see
A better day

(Many people do not understand the frustration involved in having so many divisions. Being misunderstood produces more frustration.)

They all carry pain
They all hold grief

(All parts struggle and suffer with their own memories.)

Only by splitting
Can they find relief

(The trauma within continues and builds. Further abuse and trauma causes further division, as each part finds the need to cushion the blows for the other parts.)

Yet relief does not last
So they divide again

(Eventually, the temporary cushioning of some parts by others catches up with me and the hurt in some parts are so overwhelming, they must divide into even more parts, splintering off from the others.)

While each new part
Explodes with pain

(Although each part is created to take stress off the others, they each deal with excruciating pain from their own experiences.)

These people overwhelm me
As they crowd into my soul

(It is very confusing and complicated to have many different parts all trying to do their job within me. It is almost suffocating!)

No one seems to understand
That they want to be whole

(Many people seem to believe that having more than one personality is simply a way to get attention and believe that it is only an act. But the frustration involved in this way of life causes the parts to want to integrate with one another and come out as a whole person.)

But they each must be healed
And work hand in hand

(Each part must be healed of the trauma and memories they contain. Then the various parts can work together to unite.)

Building new dreams
Out of mountains of sand

(A whole new world of possibilities opens up when the various parts can produce a whole new person and life.)

The people who have struggled
To keep my mind alive

(These inner personalities have worked to keep me sane. It has been hard work. Rather than being an indication of insanity, they actually have helped preserve sanity through each taking a part of the load of trauma.)

Have divided in my soul
To help me survive

(Not only does this dividing keep me sane, it also provides parts that can counteract the ones with suicidal tendencies.)

They deserve honor
Not ridicule or shame

(The various personalities have done a good work for me. Rather than being despised, they need to be appreciated for their contribution to the process of survival and healing.)

For they hold an identity
With or without a name

(They each have their own function with unique identities. Some have a specific name representing their role. Some do their job without a name.)

So help them heal
And comfort each one

(Please, show acceptance to the various parts, contributing to and supporting their healing.)

Until they all shine together
Like rays of the sun

(Once integrated, the parts work together as a whole unit, establishing me as one whole individual, including all that the separate parts have learned while they were divided from one another.)

A FRIEND ON THE ROAD

Sometimes along our journey
When it seems we have no friend
We stumble on the rocky road
And long for our journey to end

We don't seem to see or recognize
Others who are struggling too
While they move along the path of life
And yet reach out to you

Barely aware of their shadow
While they extend their hand
We just can't believe their concern is real
With a desire to understand

Do we think we deserve the companionship
Of those who walk quietly there?
Or do we expect a critical voice?
Or a finger to point and stare?

To trust and allow them to steady us
So we don't turn our ankle and fall
Comes from the love that we see in them
When we dare to look at them at all

A word, a smile, and the strength to share
Their faith in the journey's goal
Is just what we need to touch our life
And bring courage to our soul

We thought we were alone on our journey
Until someone helped make us aware
That they were a friend who believed in us
And could speak to our heart that they care

While walking, and yet, sometimes crawling
To arrive at my destiny
I have felt the presence of a friend with compassion
To walk on the road with me

A FRIEND ON THE ROAD (author's comments)

Sometimes along our journey
When it seems we have no friend
We stumble on the rocky road
And long for our journey to end

(While I struggled through my emotional problems and depression, I felt alone and longed for death.)

We don't seem to see or recognize
Others who are struggling too
While they move along the path of life
And yet reach out to you

(We are blind to the caring people around us. Depression blinds us to those who are concerned about us. Life is difficult for everyone in some way and yet, some people are still able to reach out to those around them with help and comfort.)

Barely aware of their shadow
While they extend their hand
We just can't believe their concern is real
With a desire to understand

(Because we don't feel confident that their love and compassion are real, we stay in denial about their presence and the outward evidence of their desire to help and understand our feelings.)

Do we think we deserve the companionship
Of those who walk quietly there?
Or do we expect a critical voice?
Or a finger to point and stare?

(Feeling unworthy of love and support, we struggle to notice that the person is not pressuring us to receive their help but quietly making it available. Instead of compassion, we expect a cruel type of criticism and the stigma and shame associated with our emotional problems.)

To trust and allow them to steady us
So we don't turn our ankle and fall
Comes from the love that we see in them
When we dare to look at them at all

(Trusting the love and concern that our companion provides for us comes from an awareness of their love whenever we come out of our mode of rejection long enough to accept it.)

A word, a smile, and the strength to share
Their faith in the journey's goal
Is just what we need to touch our life
And bring courage to our soul

(Even small gestures of friendship and encouragement go a long way in cheering someone who is depressed whether they are able to respond or not.)

We thought we were alone on our journey
Until someone helped make us aware
That they were a friend who believed in us
And could speak to our heart that they care

(The loneliness is broken by someone communicating their faith in us and their concern for us.)

While walking, and yet, sometimes crawling
To arrive at my destiny
I have felt the presence of a friend with compassion
To walk on the road with me

(Now, instead of just pondering how we all experience such friendship when we are needing it so much, I switch over to giving my own personal testimony of my experience. I describe how difficult reaching my goal to get well emotionally has been. Yet how helpful it has been for one to come beside me and comfort me along the way.)

FRIENDSHIP IS A GARDEN

Friendship is a garden
Fair and beautiful to view
And such is the garden
Of my friendship with you
Every morning, every evening
I walk beside its rows
Tending to its every need
Rejoicing as it grows
The seeds were planted by the Lord
And He provides the rain
But he asks for me to do my part
In happiness or pain
For me to walk gently beside each flower
And add to the sun my loving ray
But most of all to carefully
Pull all the weeds away
I patiently wait for each bud to bloom
So that, in haste, no petal is torn
Every sprout is tended to, no matter how small
Until its power for beauty is born
When the ground seems dry, I get a watering pail
And the water of trust I supply
As much as I can find, as much as I can sprinkle
Until new rains are sent from on high

There are times when I hoe until my back is sore
But love for the garden drives me on
I cannot rest from my loving work
Until every weed is gone
The soil so rich is made richer still
By the sweat which my labor bears
And when all else fails and the ground seems hard
I can water it with my tears
I believe in this lovely garden
Its fragrance is a comfort to me
And the honey bee never sucked pollen more sweet
Than the love each bloom offers so free
I thank God for this beautiful garden
A gift I could never repay
All I ask from Him is the strength
To tend to it day after day
No one can imagine the healing it brings
Just to know that our garden is there
And that I've been given the honor
To give it the best of my care
So allow me to love this garden
As its life comes forth complete
And spreads its vines upon the ground
Where love and friendship meet

FRIENDSHIP IS A GARDEN (author's comments)

Friendship is a garden
Fair and beautiful to view
And such is the garden
Of my friendship with you

(To see friendship as a garden, I think of its complexity and beauty. I think of flowers which grow from the heart of friendship. Love produces more love for the world to enjoy.)

Every morning, every evening
I walk beside its rows
Tending to its every need
Rejoicing as it grows

(For a friendship to succeed, each person must do maintenance. Diligent care produces the growth in the friendship which is so rewarding.)

The seeds were planted by the Lord
And He provides the rain
But he asks for me to do my part
In happiness or pain

(God, Himself, initiates our friendships with others and sends strength to help them grow. However, He gives us a job to do to help the friendship bloom into all its possibilities. Our commitment to those in our lives keeps us going in the good times or the bad.)

For me to walk gently beside each flower
And add to the sun my loving ray
But most of all to carefully
Pull all the weeds away

(Good relationships require sensitivity to other's needs. We must be gentle with one another, nurture each other in love like the sun helps flowers to grow, and more than anything else, keep strife out of our relationships.)

I patiently wait for each bud to bloom
So that, in haste, no petal is torn
Every sprout is tended to, no matter how small
Until its power for beauty is born

(Patience for the response of growth in relationships is important. If we get in too much of a hurry, damage can be done and early forcing of a response can ruin our hope of any response at all. Even small beginnings must be cared for in order for them to grow. Only in patient love can the strength be given to the plant of friendship and help it become a beautiful thing.)

When the ground seems dry, I get a watering pail
And the water of trust I supply
As much as I can find, as much as I can sprinkle
Until new rains are sent from on high

(Trust is necessary in relationships but not easy when people have been repeatedly hurt. Finding the strength to trust again so that the garden of friendship can flourish requires giving all you can give until God supplies your ability to trust with new strength.)

There are times when I hoe until my back is sore
But love for the garden drives me on
I cannot rest from my loving work
Until every weed is gone

(It is hard work to maintain a friendship well, but love continues to motivate me. I work to rid the friendship of any strife.)

The soil so rich is made richer still
By the sweat which my labor bears
And when all else fails and the ground seems hard
I can water it with my tears

(My efforts enrich the nourishment of the relationship. If the person that I am relating to develops a hard heart, I can still nurture the relationship with self-sacrifice and a willingness to suffer for their sake. My own tears and grieving can help soften the ground, which is where the roots of the relationship draw their sustenance. Often this grieving and self-sacrifice leads to prayer which does the true work of softening the ground.)

I believe in this lovely garden
Its fragrance is a comfort to me
And the honey bee never sucked pollen more sweet
Than the love each bloom offers so free

(One must have some kind of faith in friendship. The love provides comfort from any hurts of the past.)

I thank God for this beautiful garden
A gift I could never repay
All I ask from Him is the strength
To tend to it day after day

(All friendship ultimately comes from God. He provides the strength for us to do our part in cultivating the garden.)

No one can imagine the healing it brings
Just to know that our garden is there
And that I've been given the honor
To give it the best of my care

(Just having the friendship is a healing for one who has been cut off from any ability to relate to others for a long time. There is an appreciation for the entrusting of such a treasure as being able to connect to others.)

So allow me to love this garden
As its life comes forth complete
And spreads its vines upon the ground
Where love and friendship meet

(As the garden grows, it begins to connect the true meaning of love and friendship into one whole experience.)

TENDER HEART

It is your tender heart I'm needing
Your tender heart I'm longing for
When my soul is filled with grief
And my mind is filled with war
It's not your cleverness or intellect
Nor impressive words that you could say
But your soft and gentle touch
And your kind and caring way
There are no answers or solutions
That a friend could ever give
That could take the place of the love they share
And the life they help you live
So when sorrow overwhelms me
And you take me by the hand
I need your caring and compassion
Even when you don't understand
'Cause it's your tender heart that heals me
And lifts the burden that I bear
It holds me close and shields me
Showing me you really care
Your tender heart prepares me
To respond in loving ways
When it soothes and relieves me
On my tormenting, painful days
So let your tender heart be ready
To receive my love too
Because you will learn as time continues
That I have a tender heart for you

TENDER HEART (author's comments)

It is your tender heart I'm needing
Your tender heart I'm longing for
When my soul is filled with grief
And my mind is filled with war

(There is nothing so healing as the compassion coming from a tender, caring
heart. It is the ability to "weep with those who weep" which soothes those who
are hurting, mourning, and struggling with mental and spiritual warfare.)

It's not your cleverness or intellect
Nor impressive words that you could say
But your soft and gentle touch
And your kind and caring way

(Trying to come up with answers to "fix" a hurting person only alienates them
more. Instead, your gentleness and empathy brings comfort.)

There are no answers or solutions
That a friend could ever give
That could take the place of the love they share
And the life they help you live

(When people are given "pat answers" or clichés that most people have heard as
answers all of their lives, they may feel belittled as if they were too ignorant to
see the obvious answers. Helping the person have the strength to live their own
life by affirming them gives them the dignity that they need.)

So when sorrow overwhelms me
And you take me by the hand
I need your caring and compassion
Even when you don't understand

(Some people think they must understand the other's problems completely before
they can help. Understanding helps a lot but until that understanding comes,
gentle concern and kindness from a friend can go a long way.)

'Cause it's your tender heart that heals me
And lifts the burden that I bear
It holds me close and shields me
Showing me you really care

(A tender heart brings healing and lifts the burdens of rejection, shame, and low self-esteem. It protects against those who would send negative messages to me concerning what kind of person I am. Those negative words could continue to shame me if it were not for the love tenderly expressed and holding me close to others, making the reality of their love sink into my consciousness.)

Your tender heart prepares me
To respond in loving ways
When it soothes and relieves me
On my tormenting, painful days

(Your tenderness softens my own heart and helps me to show the love hidden inside of me. It does this by soothing my mind and heart so that I am free to show my emotions.)

So let your tender heart be ready
To receive my love too
Because you will learn as time continues
That I have a tender heart for you

(Prepare yourself for what I have to offer because, over time, my own tender, gentle love will come forth.)

SHEPHERD
(based on Psalm 23)

The Lord is my Shepherd but I never would have known
If someone His shepherdly love had not shown
I searched for green pastures but never could stay
For false earthly shepherds drove me away
I longed for still waters—the thirst was so deep
But the only water I found were the tears I would weep
The valley of the shadow of death was my home
Because I was forced to walk it alone
The fear and the evil were all that I knew
His rod and His staff were never in view
The comfort He wanted to bring to my soul
Was held back by tyrants who wanted control
Surely goodness and mercy are mine now at last
As I dwell in His house and conquer my past
The Shepherd who sought me has come into view
Because He could reveal Himself in you

SHEPHERD (author's comments)
(based on Psalm 23)

The Lord is my Shepherd but I never would have known
If someone His shepherdly love had not shown

(God's loving character must be shown through His called leaders. The Bible
talks about being a shepherd to His flock of people.)

I searched for green pastures but never could stay
For false earthly shepherds drove me away

(Instead of being able to find spiritual food in the various churches I attended, I
met up with rejection and condemnation which drove me from the help I was
needing.)

I longed for still waters—the thirst was so deep
But the only water I found were the tears I would weep

(I looked for a peaceful place to quench my spiritual thirst, a place that was free
from strife, turmoil, and abuse. But instead of peace, there was hurt upon hurt in
the places I would go.)

The valley of the shadow of death was my home
Because I was forced to walk it alone

(I was always living in a state of fear because I was alone and there was no one
to comfort me.)

The fear and the evil were all that I knew
His rod and His staff were never in view

(There was no comfort available from everything frightening and abusive in my
environment. Anything God had available to comfort me was never within reach
because no one revealed that comfort to me.)

The comfort He wanted to bring to my soul
Was held back by tyrants who wanted control

(Instead of serving others, the pastors I had wanted to rule in self-centered and cruel ways. There was spiritual, mental, and emotional abuse.)

Surely goodness and mercy are mine now at last
As I dwell in His house and conquer my past

(I have found a place of healing and comfort.)

The Shepherd who sought me has come into view
Because He could reveal Himself in you

(It takes people to be a channel of God's love and to reveal to others what Jesus, the Shepherd, is like.)

WHERE THE HONOR IS DUE

Let kings and queens
Find a way of their own
But honor
And place upon their throne
A lady who touches
The helpless and weak
Who gives her whole life
A child to seek

Let the strong and the wealthy
Take their hats off and bow
To the one who gives up
Her own comforts now
To comfort a child
When she needs her own sleep
Let the powerful
Look at those faces and weep
Of the precious little lambs
In the fold, in the nest
Where a woman labors
Who needs her own rest

And then let the selfish
The greedy and vain
Sit to the side
And, if they want to, complain
While the honor is given
Not to the carefree or wild
But to a woman who touches
The life of a child

WHERE THE HONOR IS DUE (author's comments)

Introduction to "Where The Honor Is Due"
     This poem was written for a woman who raised two of her own "birth children", several adopted children, and many foster children, most of whom had special needs. Her devotion to children, some in child bodies and some in adult bodies, inspired me to honor her.

Let kings and queens
Find a way of their own
But honor
And place upon their throne
A lady who touches
The helpless and weak
Who gives her whole life
A child to seek

(This is my tribute to those who minister to the lowly.)

Let the strong and the wealthy
Take their hats off and bow
To the one who gives up
Her own comforts now
To comfort a child
When she needs her own sleep
Let the powerful
Look at those faces and weep
Of the precious little lambs
In the fold, in the nest
Where a woman labors
Who needs her own rest

(No matter how powerful or rich someone is, they cannot replace someone who sacrifices her own needs to help children. Instead of boasting, the privileged should weep with compassion when they see children with any special needs.)

And then let the selfish
The greedy and vain
Sit to the side
And, if they want to, complain
While the honor is given
Not to the carefree or wild
But to a woman who touches
The life of a child

(The value God places on children makes this woman's work so noble and
blessed.)

PLEASE, LISTEN TO MY TEARS

Please, listen to my tears
For they fall with silent sound
Crying out to you
Before they touch the ground
Telling you how much I care
More than words could ever show
Longing to let you know

Please, listen to my tears
For they have messages to bring
When joined with the tears that come from you
They say, "You're not alone
For I will always sense your pain
And come faithfully as morning dew."

Please, listen to my tears
While they mingle with my prayers
Hear them echoing a love song from above
They wash all your hopes and dreams
In their gentle, cleansing streams
And bring life anew for they are liquid love

PLEASE, LISTEN TO MY TEARS (author's comments)

Please, listen to my tears
For they fall with silent sound
Crying out to you
Before they touch the ground
Telling you how much I care
More than words could ever show
Longing to let you know

(Tears say so much without making a sound. Though they are silent, we can hear their compassion if we tune in and listen.)

Please, listen to my tears
For they have messages to bring
When joined with the tears that come from you
They say, "You're not alone
For I will always sense your pain
And come faithfully as morning dew."

(The Bible says that we should "weep with those who weep". When we cry with others, they can feel the love and comfort from God, Himself, who feels our pain.)

Please, listen to my tears
While they mingle with my prayers
Hear them echoing a love song from above
They wash all your hopes and dreams
In their gentle, cleansing streams
And bring life anew for they are liquid love

(Tears are a part of intercession in prayer. They echo God's love and care. They bathe the hopes and dreams that have suffered loss, bringing a new beginning out of grief. Only love found in tears can soothe and heal like a balm.)

www.ingramcontent.com/pod-product-compliance
Lightning Source LLC
Chambersburg PA
CBHW081139290526
45795CB00006B/2303